ISLAMIC CAIRO

EGYPT
POCKET
GUIDE

Alberto Siliotti

THE AMERICAN UNIVERSITY IN CAIRO PRESS

"Al-Qahira is the metropolis of the world, the garden of the universe, the meeting place of nations, a human ant heap, the sublime site of Islam, the seat of power."

Abd el-Rahman Ibn Khaldun (1332-1406)

Text Alberto Siliotti
Photographs Claudio Concina, Alberto Siliotti
Drawings Stefania Cossu, Melissa Frigotto

English Translation Richard Pierce
General Editing Yvonne Marzoni
Graphic Design Geodia

Copyright © 2000 by Geodia (Verona, Italy)

This edition first published in Egypt jointly by
The American University in Cairo Press (Cairo and New York)
Elias Modern Publishing House (Cairo)
Geodia (Verona, Italy)

Created by Geodia (Verona, Italy)
Printed in Egypt by Elias Modern Publishing House (Cairo)
Distributed by the American University in Cairo Press (Cairo and New York)

Contents

CHRONOLOGICAL TABLE

641 d.C.	Arab Conquest of Egypt	642	Foundation of al-Fustat
661 —			
750 —	**UMAYYADS**		
		750	Foundation of al-'Askar
	ABBASIDS		
870 —	**TULUNIDS**	870	Foundation of al-Qata'i'
905 —	**IKHSHIDIDS**		
969 —			
	FATIMIDS	969	Foundation of al-Qahira
1171 —			
1250 —	**AYYUBIDS**		
			Bahri Mamluks
	MAMLUKS	1382 —	
			Burgi (Circassian) Mamluks
1517 —			
	OTTOMANS		
1798 —	Napoleon's Expedition 1798 - 1801		
1805 —	**DYNASTY OF MUHAMMAD 'ALI** British Occupation 1882 - 1954		
1952 —			

Cairo during the Ayyubid period

HISTORY

The Origins

The Tulunids

The Fatimids

The Mamluks

The Ottomans

The Origins: al-Fustat and al-'Askar

In 641 Egypt was conquered by the troops of 'Amr ibn al-'As, Khalif Omar's general. A year later, the foundation of al-Fustat marked the birth of what was to become Cairo.

The couryard and fountain of the Mosque of 'Amr ibn al-'As

'Amr ibn al-'As, the conqueror of Egypt

By order of Khalif Omar, second of the first four successors of Muhammad (*khalifa* means 'successor'), General 'Amr ibn al-'As's men conquered Egypt on 9 April 641. After a long siege against the fortress of Babylon, the country was wrested from the weakened Byzantine Empire. The following year 'Amr decided to build a permanent camp for his troops, which was the first Islamic settlement in Egypt. It was named al-Fustat, since it stood around 'Amr's tent (*fustat*), as the Arab historian and geographer al-Yaqubi wrote in 891. Next to

Attack of the Arab cavalry

the new settlement 'Amr built a mosque, the size of which increased tenfold in the next 70 years. The mosque is still being used. A little more than a century later, al-Fustat had grown over an area of 25–30 hectares, with a population of 50,000. In 750 the Abbasid khalifs from Baghdad took power from the Umayyads and founded a district north of al-Fustat called *al-'Askar*, or 'the camp,' which became the new political and administrative center, no traces of which remain.

Ibn Tulun and al-Qata'i'

The courtyard of the Mosque of Ibn Tulun

After being appointed governor of Egypt in 868, Ahmad ibn Tulun founded al-Qata'i', a dynastic city whose large mosque still stands. His descendants governed the country autonomously for 22 years.

In 868 Ahmad ibn Tulun, a military leader of Turkish origin who had lived for many years in the city of Samarra (now in Iraq), was named governor of Egypt, which he ruled until 883. In 870 he founded a new quarter called *al-Qata'i'* ('The Allotments') because the land, covering about 270 hectares, was divided into quarters that were distributed to his military followers on the basis of their ethnic origin. Ibn Tulun had his large mosque built in the middle of the new settlement, which became a dynastic city, while his palace was constructed against the Muqattam hill, not far from the spot where the Citadel

An inscription commemorating the foundation of the mosque

The sanctuary of the Mosque of Ibn Tulun

would be founded. The weakness of the Abbasid khalifate allowed Ibn Tulun to found his own dynasty, the Tulunid, which ruled Egypt until 905, when the Abbasids regained power.

The Fatimids Found al-Qahira

The Fatimid general Gawhar conquered Egypt in 969 and founded al-Qahira, 'The Victorious,' initiating a period of splendor.

Bab al-Futuh, an example of Fatimid military architecture

A Fatimid soldier

Al-Azhar, 'the Splendid,' was the first Fatimid mosque

In 969 the Fatimid khalif (so called because he was a descendant of Fatima, a daughter of Muhammad the Prophet), al-Mu'izz li-Din Allah, who lived in Tunisia, placed his 100,000 or so soldiers under the leadership of a converted Greek slave, General Gawhar al-Siqilli, and conquered Egypt, putting an end to the Abbasid dynasty and its Ikhshidid governors. At the time of this conquest al-Fustat was the economic hub of the country and one of the leading cities in the world. However, Gawhar decided to found a true imperial city, which he named *al-Qahira*, 'the Victorious,' because according to tradition the planet Mars (*al-Qahir* in Arabic) was in the ascendant during the foundation of the city. Thus began a period of great prosperity and extraordinary artistic achievements that was receptive to Byzantine, Maghrebi, and Crusader influences, a period of cultural ferment that lasted for two centuries, during which eleven khalifs ruled.

A Fatimid dish

The al-Aqmar Mosque, dating from the end of the Fatimid period, was the first to have its façade lining the street

Saladin and the Ayyubids

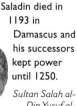

Saladin's army

*S*alah al-Din, better known as Saladin, was an ingenious and ambitious leader who succeeded in changing the fortune of Egypt and in creating a new dynasty.

The Citadel walls

The last decades of the Fatimid period were characterized by the long but weak reign of Khalif al-Mustansir (1036–94), who ascended the throne when only seven years old, as well as by an incredible number of viziers (27 from 1060 to 1066), who were appointed with the hope of overcoming serious domestic rebellion, which only Vizier Badr al-Gamali managed to quell. The siege of the city in 1168 by the troops of Amaury I of Jerusalem ended with the burning of al-Fustat and the intervention of the troops of the Sultan of Syria, Nur al-Din, who responded to Khalif al-'Adid's plea for help. These events weakened the Fatimids so much that Salah al-Din Yusuf al-Ayyubi, al-'Adid's vizier, deposed the khalif and in 1171 took power, which was recognized in 1175 by the Abbasid khalif of Baghdad. Salah al-Din, better known in the Western world as Saladin, ruled for 22 years. He reorganized the country's administration and army, restored the dominion of Sunni Islam in Egypt, and conquered Jerusalem (occupied by the Crusaders) and Syria. Saladin also introduced new institutions such as the *madrasas* (Koranic schools) and *khanqahs* (monasteries for Sufi mystics). During his reign al-Qahira was no longer merely the khalifate residence, which was its role under the Fatimids, but became a true metropolis, with over 120,000 inhabitants and occupying an area of 300 hectares (in the same period Florence covered no more than 100 hectares). Saladin was always concerned with the security of Egypt, and in order to protect himself from both the Crusaders and domestic enemies he created major defensive structures: such as the Citadel, the chief Ayyubid fortification, and the massive wall linking al-Qahira and al-Fustat.

Saladin died in 1193 in Damascus and his successors kept power until 1250.

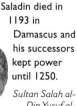

Sultan Salah al-Din Yusuf al-Ayyubi, known as Saladin

The Mamluks, Slaves and Sultans

O riginally slaves who were freed, the Mamluks were the elite troops of the last Ayyubid sultans. They took power in Egypt, ruling for 267 years.

Mamluk helmet

T oward the end of the Abbuyid dynasty the army, which once consisted of contingents of Arab tribes, was replaced by professionals who were slaves of Turkish origin and who were purch-ased, trained in military arts, and then freed. They were called Mamluks, from the Arabic word that means 'he who is owned.' The Mamluks were organized in a rigid hierarchy and in theory could not have posses-sions or occupy positions

Typical Mamluk period architecture

that were hereditary. After the death of the last Sultan, al-Salih Negm al-Din, his wife, Shagarat al-Durr, ascended the throne. But in order to retain power, she was obliged to marry again, and therefore chose al-Mu'izz Aybak as her husband in 1250. This marked the beginning of the dynasty of the Bahri Mamluks, so named because their headquarters were on the island of Roda, near the Nile (*bahr* in

Examples of Mamluk art during Sultan Qalawun's time

Arabic means 'water-course' or 'sea'). The Bahri were succeeded in 1382 by the Circassian or Burgi Mamluks. The latter were given this name because they lived in the Citadel (*burg*='tower').

A Mamluk warrior

The Ottomans

An Ottoman bey, the equivalent of a Mamluk amir

In 1517 the troops of the Ottoman sultan Selim I put an end to the Mamluk dynasty. Egypt thus lost its independence and became a province of the Ottoman Empire, remaining so until the arrival of Napoleon's army in 1798.

In the early 15th century Cairo was a large city covering an area of 450 hectares and with a population of over 150,000. But it had begun to decline inexorably, mostly because of the crisis in the Mamluk administrative system based on mercenaries, who were becoming more and more expensive and less and less efficient. On 23 January 1517 the troops of the sultan of Constantinople, Selim I, easily routed the army of Tumanbay, the successor of al-Ghuri and last Mamluk sultan, in the battle of Raydaniya, near Cairo. With this defeat Egypt became a mere province of the Ottoman Empire and Cairo lost its position as the beacon of the Islamic world.

Ottoman administration was based on a viceroy (*wali*)—who represented the central power and

Sultan Selim I

bore the title of pasha—as well as on the *beys* or princes and the janissaries, or elite troops.

An Ottoman coin

A tile from the Blue Mosque, typical of Ottoman art

The Mamhudiya Mosque, an example of Ottoman architecture

Muhammad 'Ali and His Age

Muhammad 'Ali (1805–48)

*A*ppointed pasha in 1805, Muhammad 'Ali, an Albanian mercenary, wrested Egypt from the grip of the Ottoman Empire and laid the foundations for a modern country.

Decoration of Muhammad 'Ali

The Mosque of Muhammad 'Ali in the Citadel

Muhammad 'Ali was a mere mercenary of Albanian origin who had gone to Egypt in 1801. Because of his extraordinary gifts, in only four years he managed to take power and have himself chosen as pasha. He eliminated all potential domestic opposition by annihilating what remained of Mamluk power. On 1 March 1811, he invited the Mamluk leaders (about 500 persons) to a grand banquet at the Citadel; when it was over he had them all shot to death. Muhammad 'Ali consolidated his power, with the help of his son Ibrahim Pasha, through important military moves in Sudan and Syria. Thanks to a series of basic and drastic reforms in Egyptian industry and agriculture he westernized the country, laying the foundation for modern-day Egypt. The sons and descendants of Muhammad 'Ali maintained power until 1952.

A cannon used in Muhammad 'Ali's time

ARCHITECTURE

The Mosques and Madrasas

The Sabils and Sabil-Kuttabs

The Caravanserais

Private Houses

The Mosques and Madrasas

The madrasa of Sultan Hasan

*T*he mosque is the symbol of Islam. It is the place where the faithful congregate to pray.

An elegantly decorated mihrab

Section of the mosque of Qijmas al-Ishaqi, an example of a Mamluk liwan-type mosque (with vaulted spaces) dating from the 15th century

Minaret

Dome

Mihrab: niche indicating the direction of Mecca and of prayer

Minbar: the wooden pulpit used by the officiant during prayers

Qibla: the direction of Mecca

*T*he word 'mosque' derives from the classic Arabic term masjid, which means 'place of prostration.' It is the building where the faithful gather above all for public prayers. This takes place every Friday (*yom al-jum'a* in Arabic) at noon, as is prescribed in the Quran. On this occasion the *imam*, 'he who stands in front' or 'leader,' gives his sermon from the pulpit, which is called the *minbar* in Arabic. The basic elements of a

THE MINARETS IN CAIRO

The word 'minaret' derives from the Arabic manara, or 'beacon.' This architectural element was lacking in the early mosques and first appeared in the 8th century. Naturally, the shape of the minaret varies according to the style and period, and can be roughly divided into four types: Ayyubid (A), Bahri Mamluk (B), Circassian Mamluk (C$_1$ and C$_2$), Ottoman (D).

A   B   C$_1$ C$_2$ D

Main entrance

Sanctuary

Passageway connecting the ablution area with the sanctuary

mosque are the area for ablutions where the faithful must wash their hands, face, and feet before praying; the sanctuary or prayer hall; the *mihrab*, which is the niche carved into the sanctuary wall that is the materialization of the *qibla*, or the direction of Mecca, which Muslims must face while praying; the *minbar*, which is situated to the right of the mihrab as one faces the qibla area; and the minaret. Mosques are usually of two main types of plan: *riwaq* or *liwan*. The former consists of a complex of arcades (*riwaq*) that surround a central courtyard (*sahn*), while the latter is made up of large vaulted spaces (*liwan*) that often have a cruciform plan. From the Ayyubid period on, mosques have been flanked by **madrasa**s or Quranic schools, where law and theology were taught. Sunni Islam (the doctrine that adheres to the *Sunna*, the collection of the Prophet's words and deeds) calls for four Quranic schools: Hanafi, Malaki, Shafi'i, and Hanbali.

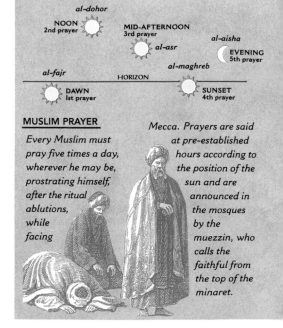

al-dohor
NOON 2nd prayer
MID-AFTERNOON 3rd prayer
al-asr
al-aisha
EVENING 5th prayer
al-fajr
HORIZON
al-maghreb
DAWN 1st prayer
SUNSET 4th prayer

MUSLIM PRAYER

Every Muslim must pray five times a day, wherever he may be, prostrating himself, after the ritual ablutions, while facing Mecca. Prayers are said at pre-established hours according to the position of the sun and are announced in the mosques by the muezzin, who calls the faithful from the top of the minaret.

The Sabils and Sabil-Kuttabs

The sabil-kuttab of Qaytbay, built in 1479

Sabils, or public fountains, are one of the most typical architectural elements in Islamic Cairo. They are often joined to a Quranic boys' school called a kuttab.

Scattered along the streets of Islamic Cairo, the *sabils* were public fountains that provided free drin 0king water to the people. Quite often the sabils, which were always on street level, had another story above them, a loggia with a *kuttab* that was connected to the sabils.

The purpose of the kuttab was to give young boys an elementary religious education. Sabils and sabil-kuttabs could be isolated structures or joined to a mosque, madrasa, or *khanqah* (a monastery for Sufi mystics). For example, the khanqah mausoleum of Farag ibn Barquq in the Northern Cemetery had two sabil-kuttabs.

Although there are sabils and sabil-kuttabs dating back to the Mamluk period, their 'golden age' was under the Ottomans: it has been calculated that no fewer than 26 were built in Cairo from 1739 to 1765, and in the early 19th century there were about 300 sabils throughout the city. Sabils were in fact monuments vested with charitable, public interest that could be built at a limited cost; consequently, those who financed them could be considered benefactors

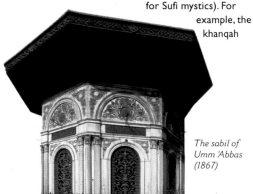

The sabil of Umm 'Abbas (1867)

of the people without really risking or locking up their assets. Among the Mamluk sabil-kuttabs, mention should be made of the extremely elegant one Sultan Qaytbay built in 1479, the first sabil not connected to any other building. One of the most beautiful and best preserved sabil-kuttabs is the one built in 1744 by 'Abd al-Rahman Katkhuda (who also had 14 other sabils built), which stands in al-Mu'izz Street.

A tile that decorated the sabil-kuttab of Katkhuda

Section of the sabil-kuttab of 'Abd al-Rahman Katkhuda, built in 1744, during the Ottoman period

Hollow space to improve insulation

Loggia used as a **kuttab**, or Quranic school for boys

Main entrance

Walls decorated with tiles

Sabil or public fountain

The Caravanserais (Wikala)

The inner courtyard of the wikala of al-Ghuri. It was built in 1504 and is the best-preserved caravanserai in Cairo

Caravanserais, called khan *or* wikala *in Arabic, were structures built as lodgings in the city for merchants and their caravans.*

The caravanserais were true institutions in the Islamic world because they were the basis of the closely woven network of commercial transactions connected to the great caravan routes. Known as *khans* in the Mamluk period and *wikalas* under the Ottomans, the caravanserais were built to provide hospitality to the passing caravans—the animals were kept on the ground floor together with the goods placed in the warehouse, while the merchants were given accommodation in the upper floors, in the section called *rab'a*. The lodgings were structured as small

Traveling Arab merchants

The portal-entrance of the wikala of Qaytbay

independent units, each with a kitchen and bathrooms. The wikala, which to a certain extent could be considered the precursor of inns and modern-day hotels, provided accommodation to travelers, foreign residents, and military troops and was also the

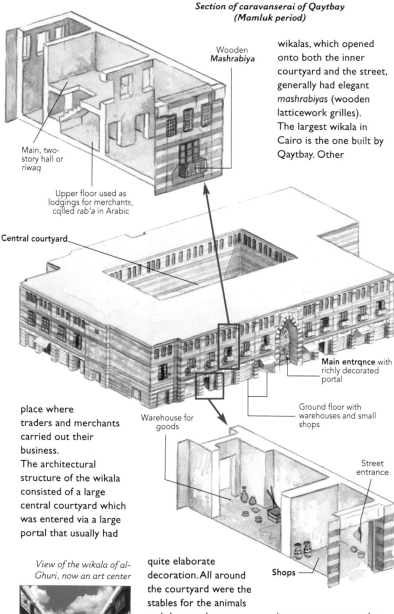

Section of caravanserai of Qaytbay
(Mamluk period)

Wooden *Mashrabiya*

Main, two-story hall or *riwaq*

Upper floor used as lodgings for merchants, called *rab'a* in Arabic

Central courtyard

Main entrance with richly decorated portal

Ground floor with warehouses and small shops

Warehouse for goods

Street entrance

Shops

View of the wikala of al-Ghuri, now an art center

wikalas, which opened onto both the inner courtyard and the street, generally had elegant *mashrabiyas* (wooden latticework grilles). The largest wikala in Cairo is the one built by Qaytbay. Other place where traders and merchants carried out their business. The architectural structure of the wikala consisted of a large central courtyard which was entered via a large portal that usually had quite elaborate decoration. All around the courtyard were the stables for the animals and the warehouses where goods were stored; the latter also opened out to the street in order to serve as shops as well. The windows in the important ones are the wikala of al-Ghuri (1504) and the wikala of Oda Bashi (1673), which was the center of spices and coffee commerce.

Private Houses

The qa'a *in the Bayt al-Kritliya, with the* durqa'a *and the* fasqiya

*I*n Cairo most of the private houses date from the Ottoman period. Several of them are masterworks of domestic architecture, some of which have been restored recently.

*T*he plan of private houses (called *bayt* in Arabic) in Cairo varies, but the structure always centers around a large hall called the *qa'a*, which is the hub of famly life and at times is also used as a reception hall, though guests were often received in the *maq'ad*, a loggia that one could enter from the courtyard below. The qa'a had a central section on a lower level called the *durqa'a*; in the middle was a fountain or *fasqiya* and, between the ceiling and roof, there was a polygonal structure, or *shukhsheikha*, which provided light. Ventilation in the main hall was afforded by a device called the *malqaf*, which was a sort of windcatcher. Some of the most important private houses (Bayt Mustafa Ga'far and above all the large Bayt al-Sihaymi) are located in Darb al-Asfar Street, which opens into al-Mu'izz Street. They were recently restored and have thus regained their former splendor. The beautiful Bayt al-Kritliya is the Gayer-Anderson Museum.

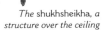

The shukhsheikha, *a structure over the ceiling*

The Bayt Dahabi entrance

THE GREAT MONUMENTS

The Mosque of Ibn Tulun

The Mosque of al-Hakim

The Mosque of al-Azhar

The Madrasa of Sultan Hasan

The Mosque of Muhammad 'Ali

The Mosque of Ibn Tulun

*T*his mosque is not only the oldest in Cairo that has survived intact to this day, but is the only remaining part of al-Qata'i', the Tulunid citadel.

The spiral minaret

The large courtyard of the Mosque of Ibn Tulun with the fountain for ablutions

*T*he mosque of Ibn Tulun was built in 876–879 on Yashkur hill. It was the religious center of al-Qata'i', the dynastic military citadel founded by Ahmad ibn Tulun and, together with al-Fustat and al-'Askar, was the nucleus of present-day Cairo. The mosque, designed by a Christian architect, covers an area of over three hectares. The harmonious proportions of its volumes and refined decoration make it one of the masterpieces of Islamic architecture.

The edifice is made entirely of red bricks covered with a layer of stucco. It is a typical example of a porticoed mosque that runs around a large central courtyard, in the middle of which is the fountain for ablutions. The courtyard is surrounded by four *riwaqs* or arcades consisting of a double row of arches and a back wall with 128 windows, each of which bears particular decoration. The chief riwaq is the east one, commonly called the *qibla*, oriented

Crenellation decoration on the outer wall of the mosque

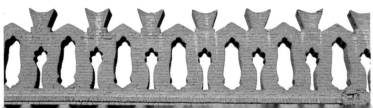

The sanctuary of the mosque

toward Mecca. It consists of five orders of arches and is the sanctuary proper that houses the *mihrab* (the niche, usually elaborately decorated, that faces Mecca and is the materialization of the qibla) and the *minbar* or pulpit from which the *imam* (officiant) gives the sermon (*khutba*) during Friday noon prayer. The minbar is made of finely carved wood and dates from 1296, when it was donated to the mosque by the sultan Husam al-Din Lagin, who restored the mosque and had the fountain built in the middle of the central courtyard. The back wall of the sanctuary is decorated with a long inscription with Quranic verses in Kufic script. The mosque, which has virtually no façade, is surrounded on three sides (north, south, and west) by an empty space called the *ziyada*, which in turn is surrounded by a tall wall with nineteen doors that isolates the mosque from the outside world. On the west side of the ziyada is a spiral minaret, this time not made of bricks but of blocks of stone. The shape of this minaret is unique in Cairo mosques, which has led scholars to believe that Ibn Tulun drew inspiration from the Great Mosque at Samarra, in Iraq. The finial (ornament) on the top of the miaret dates back to the restorations effected by Husam. It was built in the *mabkhara* ('incense pot') style.

Plan of the Mosque of Ibn Tulun

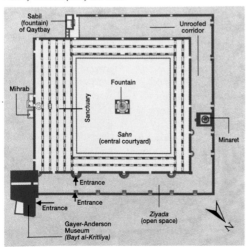

The Gayer-Anderson Museum

Islamic Cairo Map

C3

A large room in the Gayer-Anderson Museum

*M*ajor Gayer-Anderson of the British Army had an important collection of Islamic objects that in 1937 was exhibited in an old house known as Bayt al-Kritliya situated next to the Mosque of Ibn Tulun.

On one side of the Mosque of Ibn Tulun is a house built in 1631 and named the 'House of

One of the finely inlaid mashrabiya screens that decorate the façade

the Cretan Woman' (Bayt al-Kritliya) because it was purchased, perhaps in the early 19th century, by a lady from the Greek island. Next to it there is another house dating from 1540 called the house of Amna bint Salim al-Gazzar ('Amna, daughter of the butcher Salim'). The two houses were later joined and they now house the beautiful collection of furniture and art and handicraft objects collected by the British Army major and physician, Robert Gayer-Anderson (1881–1945),

who was given the title of pasha for merit. He lived in the House of the Cretan Woman until 1942, having himself restored and furnished it.

View of the courtyard

The al-Ghuri Complex

The last masterpiece of Mamluk art, the complex built by Sultan Qansuh al-Ghuri, also known as 'the Ghuriya', is the expression of highly refined architecture.

A whirling dervish

Sultan al-Ghuri's mausoleum

Sultan al-Ghuri was the penultimate Mamluk ruler (1501–16), who died in battle against the Ottoman Turks near Aleppo. His complex lies a few hundred meters from the al-Azhar Mosque and is made up of a mosque-madrasa and a mausoleum with a sabil-kuttab annexed to it. They were built in 1501–05 opposite each other at the southern end of al-Mu'izz Street

The al-Ghuri caravanserai

(also called at this point al-Ghuriya Street). The mosque-madrasa has a cruciform plan with four liwans and is elegantly decorated with polychrome marble. The distinguishing feature of the recently restored mausoleum, which houses the tomb of al-Ghuri's successor, al-Ashraf Tumanbay, is its unfinished dome. There is also a large hall that was transformed into a theater where performances based on the famous whirling dervishes are given. The

original dervishes are members of an ascetic religious order who achieve ecstasy by means of a dance in which they whirl around at breakneck speed. Near the mausoleum, al-Ghuri built a large caravanserai or *wikala* that has been restored and is now a cultural and art center.

Al-Ghuri's mosque

The Mosque of al-Azhar

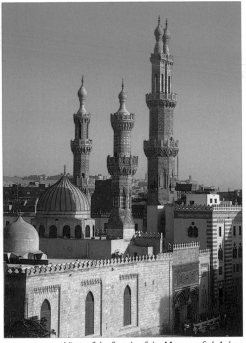

View of the façade of the Mosque of al-Azhar

Al-Azhar, 'the splendid,' was the first mosque built by the founder of Cairo and military leader, Gawhar al-Siqilli. Construction was finished in 972 and over the centuries the mosque was drastically rebuilt. It now houses the most important Quranic university in the world.

The mosque was the most important edifice in Fatimid Cairo, since the power of the khalifs was religious and the mosque symbolized both their submission to Allah and their absolute authority on this earth. Work on the Mosque of al-Azhar began in 969 at the behest of al-Gawhar and ended three years later. The original building covered an area of slightly less than 6,000 square meters and

The immense sanctuary measures 4,000 square meters

Madrasa of Aqbugha

consisted of a *riwaq* mosque, that is, with arcaded aisles surrounding a central courtyard (*sahn*) measuring 1,632 square meters, with the sanctuary of five parallel aisles, similar to the Mosque of Ibn Tulun. The mosque was drastically rebuilt and enlarged several times, especially in the second half of the 18th century on the part of 'Abd al-Rahman Katkhuda, an Ottoman janissary commander and influential figure in Cairo. From the outset the Mosque of al-Azhar was a center of law and theology studies, and can be considered the oldest university in the world. Its cultural inclination and tradition have made it the leading school of Quranic studies in the Islamic world. It now has over 85,000 students who take courses in nine faculties. The university library has 60,000 books and 15,000 manuscripts.

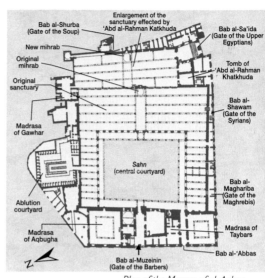

Plan of the Mosque of al-Azhar

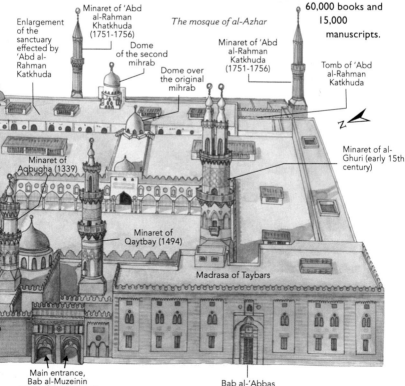

The mosque of al-Azhar

The Mosque of al-Hakim

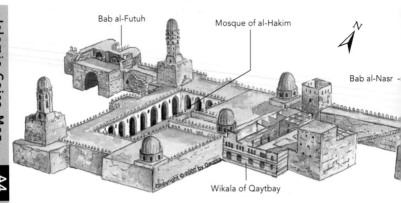

Bab al-Futuh

Mosque of al-Hakim

Bab al-Nasr

Wikala of Qaytbay

The great mosque of al-Hakim

*L*ying between the two large monumental gates of Bab al-Futuh and Bab al-Nasr, the Mosque of al-Hakim is the second oldest Fatimid mosque in Cairo after al-Azhar. Abandoned for centuries and used for different purposes, the mosque was completely restored in 1981.

Al-'Aziz, the fifth Fatimid khalif, who reigned from 975 to 996, began construction work in 990 on a large mosque situated in the northern section of the city. The building originally lay outside the city walls built by al-Gawhar. It was later enclosed by the massive walls built by Badr al-Din al-Gamali, vizier of Khalif al-Mustansir (1035–94), who extended al-Gawhar's walls so that Cairo became larger, covering an area of 160 hectares, a size it maintained until 1798. Al-Gawhar also built two large monumental gates to the east and west of

The walls built by Badr al-Din al-Gamali in 1087–91

the mosque—*Bab al-Futuh* (Gate of Conquests) and *Bab al-Nasr* (Gate of Victory)—which were designed by three Syrian architects from Edessa, who were brothers. The mosque was finished in 1013 by al-'Aziz's son, al-Hakin bi-Amr Allah (996–1021), who ascended the throne at the age of eleven and soon became notorious for his religious intolerance, ferocious mania for persecution, and many eccentricities (for example, in order to oblige women to stay home he

The central courtyard of the Mosque of al-Hakim

prohibited cobblers from making women's shoes), which earned him the epithet of 'the Caligula of Islam.' The plan of this

the north and south corners of the façade, mark an innovation in Fatimid architecture. Originally the minaret in the north corner had a cylindrical section, while the south one was

Baybars II al-Gashankir (1308–10). The Mosque of al-Hakim met a strange fate. At first it was converted into a prison, then became a large stable during the Ayyubid period and a fortress for Napoleon's troops. In the early 19th century it had fallen into ruins, but in 1890 it was again utilized, this time as a repository for Islamic art objects. Lastly, during Nasser's presidency part of the mosque was used as a school. The Mosque of al-Hakim was virtually rebuilt in 1980–81 by the Bohras, an Islamic sect based in India.

Bab al-Nasr, the Gate of Victory, was built in 1087 along the lines of Greco-Roman architecture.

grandiose porticoed mosque around a central courtyard, which covered an area of 25,000 square meters, seems to have been inspired by the Mosque of Ibn Tulun. However, there is a distinct difference. The shape and position of the two minarets, which have *mabkhara* ('incense pot') finials and are located at

quadrangular. Later on, in 1010, for reasons unknown, al-Hakim had the minarets incorporated into the truncated pyramidal structures, giving them their unusual look, much like the towers of a fortress. The minarets were seriously damaged by an earthquake in 1303 and were restored by Sultan

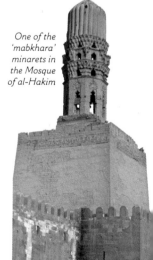

One of the 'mabkhara' minarets in the Mosque of al-Hakim

Khan al-Khalili

*T*he Khan al-Khalili is not only the largest bazaar in the entire Near East as well as a colorful spectacle, but is also one of the richest and most interesting monumental quarters in Cairo, a must for anyone visiting the Egyptian capital.

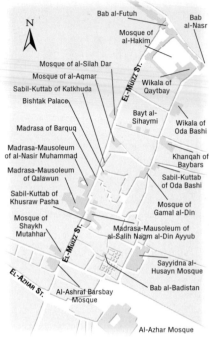

Plan of the Khan al-Khalili and the north monumental zone

The minaret of al-Salih Nagm al-Din Ayyub

*T*he nucleus of the Khan al-Khalili lies between the al-Husayn mosque and al-Mu'izz li-Din Allah Street, which corresponds to the main thoroughfare in Cairo during the Fatimid period, which, going in a north–south direction, connected the Bab al-Futuh and present-day Bab Zuwayla gates. Khan al-Khalili was given this name because it was orginally a complex of caravanserais (which at that time were called *khans*, and under the Ottoman Turks *wikalas*)

that was built in 1382, during the reign of Sultan Barquq, by the amir Jarkas al-Khalili in the area that was then occupied by the tombs of the Fatimid khalifs, all traces of which have since disappeared.

Al-Mu'izz Street

The Khan al-Khalili soon became very important and in 1511 Sultan al-Ghuri had it rebuilt after tearing down the earlier structures. The Khan al-Khalili continued to grow throughout the Mamluk age with the addition of new caravanserais, and monumental buildings

Spices on sale at the bazaar

emporium. On al-Mu'izz li-Din Allah Street, the main artery in the quarter, there are also many fine monuments: the mosque of Sultan al-Ashraf Barsbay, built in 1425; the mosque of Sheikh Mutahhar; the madrasa of Sultan Salih Nagm al-Din Ayyub (1241–44), the only remains of which is the gate with a characteristic Ayyubid minaret on its top; and further down the street, the same sultan's mausoleum.

Façade of the al-Ashraf Barsbay mosque

were added. It then went through a period of considerable decine under the Ottomans, only to regain its former splendor with the rise to power of Muhammad 'Ali. Today the enormous amount of buying and selling that lends such vitality to the bazaar is divided into different sectors according to the type of goods offered. Thus visitors can

distinguish an area for merchants trading in gold and jewels, another one given over to perfumes or spices, and so forth. However, Khan al-Khalili is not only a huge

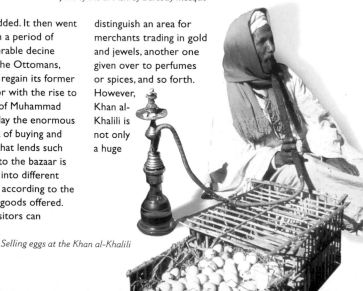

Selling eggs at the Khan al-Khalili

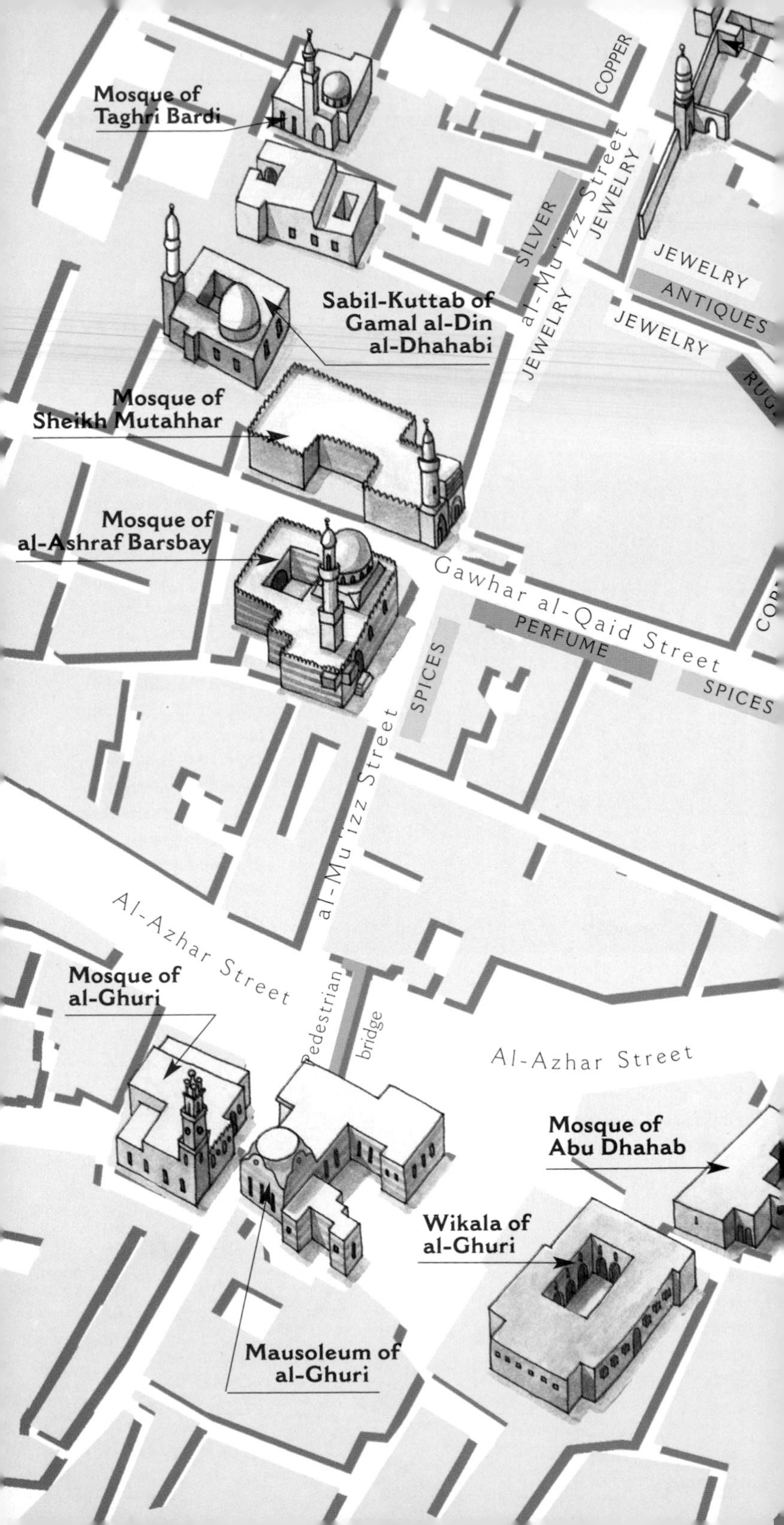

Mosque of Taghri Bardi

COPPER

Sabil-Kuttab of Gamal al-Din al-Dhahabi

SILVER

al-Mu'izz Street

JEWELRY

JEWELRY

JEWELRY

ANTIQUES

JEWELRY

RUG

Mosque of Sheikh Mutahhar

Mosque of al-Ashraf Barsbay

Gawhar al-Qaid Street

COPPER

PERFUME

SPICES

SPICES

al-Mu'izz Street

Al-Azhar Street

Mosque of al-Ghuri

Pedestrian bridge

Al-Azhar Street

Mosque of Abu Dhahab

Wikala of al-Ghuri

Mausoleum of al-Ghuri

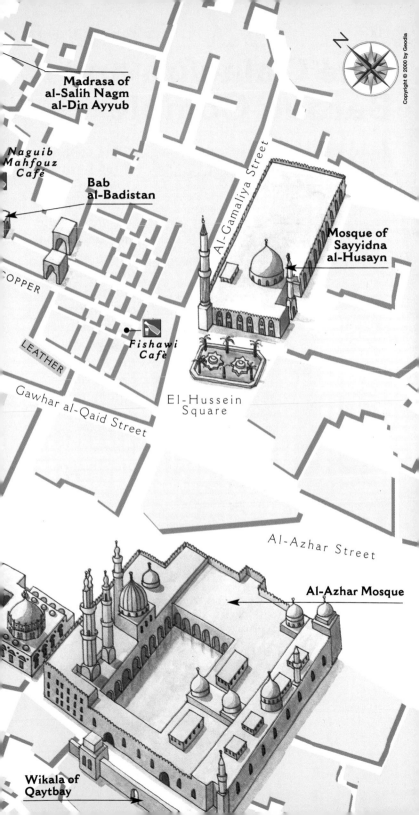

Madrasa of
al-Salih Nagm
al-Din Ayyub

Naguib
Mahfouz
Café

Bab
al-Badistan

COPPER

LEATHER

Fishawi
Cafè

Gawhar al-Qaid Street

Al-Gamaliya Street

Mosque of
Sayyidna
al-Husayn

El-Hussein
Square

Al-Azhar Street

Al-Azhar Mosque

Wikala of
Qaytbay

Copyright © 2000 by Geodia

The Qalawun and Barquq Complexes

Detail of the façade of Qalawun's mausoleum

The complexes of Sultans Qalawun, al-Nasir, and Barquq are the most important monuments, from an artistic point of view, in the entire monumental area north of the Khan al-Khalili and among the greatest achievements of Islamic architecture.

The grandiose complexes of the sultans Qalawun, al-Nasir Muhammad, and Barquq are situated on the western side of al-Mu'izz Street in a district known as *Bayn al-Qasrayn*, 'between the two palaces,' alluding to the fact that it once lay between the two royal palaces that were the nerve center of the city during the Fatimid period.

Al-Mansur Qalawun, who reigned from 1279 to 1290, was the first sultan to build a monumental complex, which included a large hospital (*bimaristan*) that

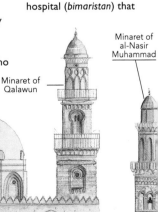

The monumental complexes of Qalawun, al-Nasir Muhammad, and Barquq

Madrasa of Qalawun

Sabil of al-Nasir Muhammad

Qalawun's mausoleum

Minaret of Qalawun

Minaret of al-Nasir Muhammad

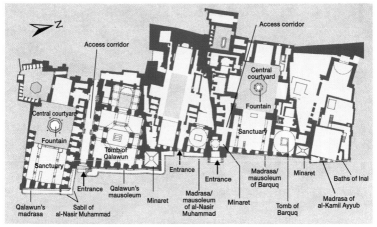

Plan of the Bayn al-Qasrayn area with Qalawun's, al-Nasir's, and Barquq's monuments

could accommodate up to 4,000 patients per day

ruled for **47** years (1293–1340), built next

war booty taken from a Christian church at Acre. Sultan al-Zahir Barquq (1382–99), the founder of the Circassian Mamluk dynasty, built his monumental complex next to al-Nasir's mausoleum. This too consisted of a madrasa and a mausoleum.

The tomb of Sultan Qalawun inside his mausoleum

The famous Gothic doorway of the al-Nasir Muhammad complex

(unfortunately very little of the original structure has survived) and a madrasa, to which was annexed a large mausoleum that houses the tomb of Qalawun. Later on, in 1304, Sultan al-Nasir Muhammad, Qalawun's son, who

to his father's complex a madrasa and a mausoleum whose Gothic portal was

The Madrasa of Sultan Hasan

Built in 1356–63 at the foot of the Citadel, the madrasa-mausoleum of Sultan al-Nasir Hasan is the largest medieval religious monument in Islam and one of the masterpieces of Islamic architecture.

The madrasa of Sultan Hasan seen from al-Qal'a Square

Sultan al-Malik al-Nasir Hasan, the seventh son of al-Nasir Muhammad, ascended the throne in 1347 at the age of thirteen and, after being deposed by one of his brothers, regained power in 1354. Two years later Hasan began construction work on his madrasa, which lasted seven years. This gigantic edifice with a total area of 10,200 square meters has a cruciform plan with four liwans opening onto the central courtyard (*sahn*). The courtyard measures 1,152 square meters and has a large fountain in the middle for ablutions crowned by a dome. Four madrasas were built at the four corners of the building—named the Shafi'i, Hanafi, Hanbali, and Maliki, after the four rites of Sunni Islam—and each one has its own entrance door and courtyard.

The main liwan, which opens onto the qibla side of the building, has a wide vault from which 70 chains still hang; they originally held oil lamps, some of which are now kept in the Cairo Islamic Museum. In the middle of the liwan is an impressive marble *dikka* (platform) supported by three pillars and a double row of four columns, in front of the

The mihrab in the Sultan Hasan madrasa

Detail of the elaborate decoration in the madrasa

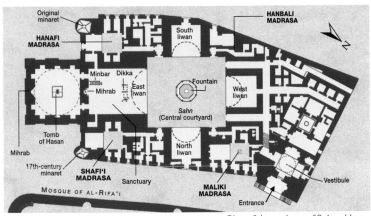

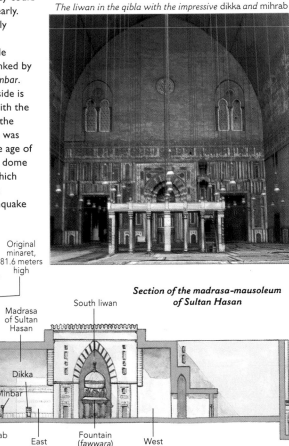

Plan of the madrasa of Sultan Hasan

mihrab: this pulpit was occupied by a person who repeated the words of the *imam* so they could be heard more clearly. The mihrab is finely decorated with polychrome marble paneling and is flanked by a white marble *minbar*. Beyond the qibla side is the mausoleum, with the tomb of Hasan in the middle (the sultan was assassinated at the age of 26), crowned by a dome 28 meters high, which collapsed during a tremendous earthquake in 1660 and was reconstructed by the Ottomans. The original minaret, on the southwest corner, is the tallest in Islamic Cairo: 81.6 meters.

The liwan in the qibla with the impressive dikka and mihrab

Section of the madrasa-mausoleum of Sultan Hasan

The Mosque of al-Mu'ayyad

*T*his complex of Sultan al-Mu'ayyad was built in 1415–20 to fulfill a vow and became an important academic institution in the 15th century.

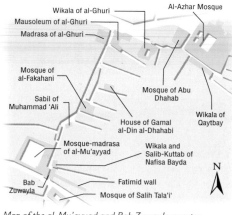

Wikala of al-Ghuri
Mausoleum of al-Ghuri
Madrasa of al-Ghuri
Al-Azhar Mosque
Mosque of al-Fakahani
Mosque of Abu Dhahab
Sabil of Muhammad 'Ali
House of Gamal al-Din al-Dhahabi
Wikala of Qaytbay
Mosque-madrasa of al-Mu'ayyad
Wikala and Salib-Kuttab of Nafisa Bayda
Bab Zuwayla
Fatimid wall
Mosque of Salih Tala'i'
N

Map of the al-Mu'ayyad and Bab Zuwayla quarter

Sultan al-Mu'ayyad reigned from 1412 to 1421 and in 1415 began construction of his monumental complex, which consists of a mosque, a madrasa, and a mausoleum. The great Arab historian al-Maqrizi relates that when al-Mu'ayyad was still an amir before becoming sultan, he was put in a terrible prison because of court intrigues he was plotting. He vowed that if he were ever to become

Bab Zuwayla and the minarets of the Mosque of al-Mu'ayyad

The bronze doors of the Mosque of al-Mu'ayyad

sultan he would build a mosque in place of the prison, which he did three years after he ascended the throne. The mosque-madrasa became a leading academic and cultural institution in the

Polychrome decoration on the frame of the entrance door of the mosque of al-Mu'ayyad

is the magnificent and exquisitely decorated bronze portal, which originally belonged to the madrasa of Sultan Hasan. On either side of the portal, whose jambs are decorated with polychrome patterns, is an inscription in Kufic script carved into the marble that quotes the basic credo of Muslims: "There is no god but Allah and Muhammad is his Prophet."

The two minarets of the mosque are identical and were built above the towers of the south gate of the Fatimid wall, known as Bab Zuwayla, which dates back to 1092 and was named after the soldiers who belonged to the Berber Zawila tribe.

The architect, Muhammad ibn al-Qazzaz, had his name and the date of construction (1421 and 1422) carved at

Al-Mu'ayyad mosque from a drawing by the French architect Pascal Coste (1787-1879)

Kufic inscription at the entrance of the al-Mu'ayyad Mosque

15th century and boasted a fine library. The façade of the al-Mu'ayyad complex is dominated by the large dome that towers over the sultan's mausoleum, which also houses the tomb of his son Ibrahim. In the façade

the entrance of each minaret, the only case of this kind in the history of Mamluk architecture. From the platform on top of the gate between the two minarets the Mamluk sultans used to watch the passage of the *mahmal*, the caravan that initiated the pilgrimage to Mecca.

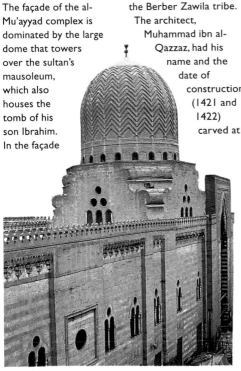

Façade of the Mosque of al-Mu'ayyad

The Blue Mosque

*T*he Mosque of Aqsunqur, better known as the 'Blue Mosque' because of the splendid tiles that decorate the qibla wall, is a hidden gem of Islamic architecture.

The courtyard and minaret of the Blue Mosque

Shams al-Din Aqsunqur, who was amir and Sultan al-Nasir Muhammad's master of the hunt as well as his son-in-law, built his mosque in 1347 along the eastern side of Bab al-Wazir Street, putting his plain, austere tomb inside.

This mosque is based on a plan with a central courtyard (*sahn*) surrounded by four arcades (*riwaq*). In the middle of the courtyard, palm trees mark the remains of the ablution fountain built by Amir Thugan in 1412. The mosque also became the mausoleum of Sultan al-

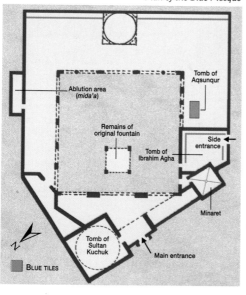

Plan of the Blue Mosque

- Ablution area (*mida'a*)
- Tomb of Aqsunqur
- Remains of original fountain
- Tomb of Ibrahim Agha
- Side entrance
- Minaret
- Tomb of Sultan Kuchuk
- Main entrance

■ BLUE TILES

Main entrance

Ashraf Kuchuk, the eighth son of Sultan al-Nasir Muhammad, who ascended the throne in 1351 at the age of six and ruled for only five months before being

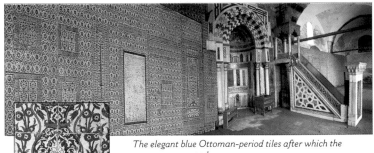

The elegant blue Ottoman-period tiles after which the mosque was named

imprisoned in the Citadel and strangled to death at the behest of his brother, officer. It was then that the magnificent blue tiles with their floral motifs, a characteristic feature of Ottoman decoration during this period, were marble minbar (pulpit) with geometric polychrome decoration. Other blue tiles of the same kind also decorate part of the tomb of Ibrahim Agha, which lies at the southwest corner of the mosque and is made of precious Italian marble. In the same corner is the minaret,

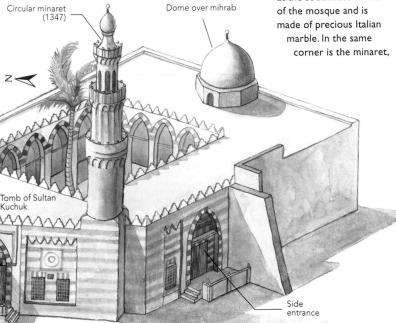

Circular minaret (1347)

Dome over mihrab

Z

Tomb of Sultan Kuchuk

Side entrance

The Blue Mosque viewed from Bab al-Wazir Street

Sultan Sha'ban. Under the Ottomans, in 1652–54, the mosque was usurped and redecorated by Ibrahim Agha Mustahfizan, a top army added to the mosque and gave it its name. The tiles were probably imported from Damascus and are on the wall of the qibla, which also boasts a rare built in 1347 and characterized by its circular shaft, which retains this shape from the base to the top.

The Citadel

*A*l-Qal'a, or the Citadel, the massive fortress dominating Cairo, is the most popular Islamic monument with tourists and includes museums, palaces, and three mosques, the most famous of which is the mosque of Muhammad 'Ali.*

The Mosque of Muhammad 'Ali viewed from the south

The Citadel was built in 1176 on a spur of the Muqattam hill by Sultan Salah al-Din Yusuf Ayyubi (Saladin) to defend the city from the Crusaders and later became the residence of the Mamluk sultans. The first major mosque in the Citadel was built under Sultan al-Nasir Muhammad in 1318–35. Two other mosques were erected in the Ottoman period by Sulayman Pasha (1528) and Muhammad 'Ali. The Mosque of Muhammad 'Ali was built along the lines of

The tomb of Muhammad 'Ali

Turkish architecture in 1824–57 and completely covered with alabaster slabs, which earned it the nickname of 'alabaster mosque.' It is

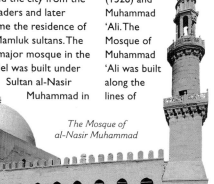

The Mosque of al-Nasir Muhammad

The internal courtyard of the Mosque of Muhammad 'Ali with the ablution fountain and clock

has a large clock that was given to Muhammad 'Ali in 1846 by King Louis Philippe of France. Muhammad also built other works within the Citadel walls, such as the Gawhara Palace and Harim Palace (now the Military Museum), by changing the original

undoubtedly the most impressive building in the Citadel and has become the monument-symbol of Cairo. Inside this mosque, which has a huge dome flanked by four semi-domes, is Muhammad 'Ali's tomb. The eastern section of the mosque courtyard

The sanctuary hall in the Mosque of Muhammad 'Ali

The domes of the Mosque of Muhammad 'Ali

structures in the enclosure rather drastically. The complex has remained the same ever since.

In the second half of the 19th century the Citadel became a barracks and was used as such by British troops until 1946.

Plan of the Mosque of Muhammad 'Ali

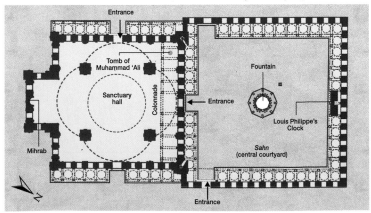

Entrance

Tomb of Muhammad 'Ali

Sanctuary hall

Colonnade

Fountain

Entrance

Louis Philippe's Clock

Mihrab

Sahn (central courtyard)

Entrance

The Tombs of the Mamluks

A lso known as the Northern Cemetery, this vast necropolis north of the Citadel and at the foot of the Muqattam hills contains marvelous examples of Islamic architecture.

The mausoleum of Sultan al-Ashraf Qaytbay

T he Northern Cemetery, so named because of its location north of the Citadel, has two other names, 'Tombs of the Mamluks' and 'Tombs of the Khalifs,' although this latter name is erroneous. This is the most important monumental cemetery in Cairo and some of its mausoleums, in which five sultans of the Circassian Mamluk dynasty are buried, are masterpieces of Islamic art and architecture. Among the most outstanding monuments, mention should be made of the complex of Qurqumas,

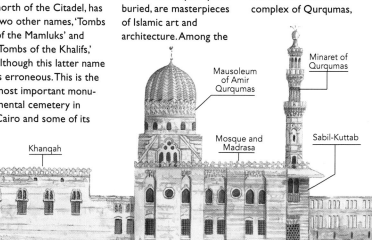

Khanqah

Mausoleum of Amir Qurqumas

Minaret of Qurqumas

Mosque and Madrasa

Sabil-Kuttab

View of the complex of Farag ibn Barquq

are the twin minarets, domes, and sabil-kuttabs. It also has a *khanqah* (a sort of convent for Sufi holy men). In the sanctuary proper—at the sides of which are the tombs of the sultan, his children, and his wives and hand-maidens—there is a splendidly carved minbar.

who was amir during the reign of Sultan al-Ghuri (1501–16). Besides the mausoleum, it contains a mosque-madrasa, a sabil-kuttab and a section with lodgings. Next to this complex is the less impressive one of Sultan Inal (1453–60).

But the real gem in this monumental cemetery is the complex of Sultan al-Ashraf Qaytbay (1468–96), which includes the mausoleum as well as a madrasa whose elegance and perfect proportions combine with extremely rich and refined decoration.

Another architectural jewel is the complex of Sultan Farag ibn Barquq

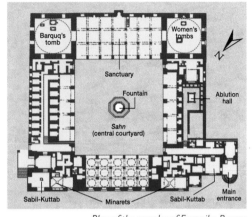

Plan of the complex of Farag ibn Barquq

(1399–1405), the son of Barquq, who founded the Circassian Mamluk dynasty. This is the largest complex in the Northern Cemetery, with an area of over 4,600 square meters. The distinguishing feature of this structure

The courtyard of Farag ibn Barquq's mausoleum

The complexes of Qurqumas and Inal

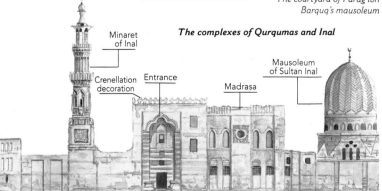

The Nilometer

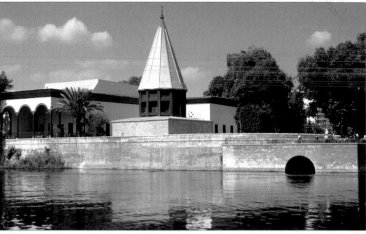

The Nilometer on the island of Roda has a 19th-century pointed roof

*S*ituated on the island of Roda in a calm and charming place off the beaten tourist track, the Nilometer is the oldest Islamic monument in Cairo that has survived practically intact.

The interior of the Nilometer

For millennia Egypt lived according to the rhythm of the Nile and its periodic flood, which occurred from July to September. From pharaonic times the river level was measured by the so-called nilometers, wells dug into the ground with a graduated column that made it possible to measure the height of the water with a great degree of accuracy and gauge the extent of the flood.

In 861, the Abbasid khalif al-Mutawakkil had a nilometer (*miqyas* in Arabic, 'measure') built at the southernmost end of the island of Roda in Cairo, and most of its original structure has survived to this day.

The Nilometer in a drawing by the artist Luigi Mayer: in the middle is the column graduated in cubits that made it possible to determine the exact height of the river

The Museum of Islamic Art

*T*his museum houses one of the finest and most interesting collections of Islamic art in the world, with over 75,000 pieces.

A ninth-century ivory box from Andalusia

The Museum of Islamic Art

Islamic Cairo Map

B3

A rare double-pointed saber

*T*he Museum of Islamic Art was inaugurated in 1903 in a section of a large building on Port Said Street that was also the home of the National Library (Dar al-Kutub). The collections are mounted in 23 halls and arranged according to the style and medium of the objects. For example, one hall is given over to metal objects, another one to objects made of wood and ivory. Among the finest collections are the arms and armor and the ceramics (on display in three rooms); among other things, the latter includes some of loveliest panels that adorned the Blue Mosque. Another very interesting section features manuscripts, where visitors can admire Mamluk and Ottoman illuminated manuscripts and splendid illuminated editions of the Quran. One room is given over to Arab medicine, while another has on display highly elegant wooden inlay work dating to the Fatimid period.

Ottoman illuminated manuscript

ESSENTIAL BIBLIOGRAPHY

Antoniou, J., *Historic Cairo: A Walk through the Islamic City*. Cairo, 1998.
Blue Guide Egypt. London & New York, 1983.
Behrens-Abouseif, D., *The Minarets of Cairo*. Cairo, 1985.
Coste, P., *Architecture arabe, Monuments du Kaire*. Paris, 1839.
Creswell, K.A.C., *Architecture of Muslim Egypt*. Oxford, 1952–59.
Kubiak, W.B., *Al-Fustat: Its Foundation and Early Urban Development*. Cairo, 1987.
Lyster, W., *The Citadel of Cairo*. Cairo, 1990.
Maqrizi, *Histoire des sultans mamelouks de l'Égypte*. Paris, 1832.
Robinson, F., *The Cambridge Illustrated History of the Islamic World*, Cambridge. 1996.
Prisse D'Avennes, A.C., *L'Art arabe*. Paris, 1877.
Ravéreau, A., M. Roche, *Le Caire, esthétique et tradition*. Paris, 1997.
Raymond, A., *Le Caire*. Paris, 1993.
Raymond, A., *Le Caire des Janissaires*. Paris 1995.
Siliotti, A., *The Discovery of Ancient Egypt*. Vercelli, 1998.
Stierlin, H. and A., *L'Égypte des Mille et une Nuits*. Paris, 1996.
Wiet, G., *Les mosquées du Caire*. Cairo, 1996.
Williams, C., *Islamic Monuments in Cairo: A Practical Guide*. Cairo, 1993.

PHOTOGRAPH CREDITS

DRAWINGS